THE Great LAKES

by
LINDA THOMPSON

Rourke
Publishing LLC
Vero Beach, Florida 32964

www.rourkepublishing.com

PHOTO CREDITS:
Courtesy U.S. Army, Center of Military History: pages 36, 41; Courtesy Library of Congress, Edward S. Curtis Collection: page 17; Courtesy Library of Congress, Prints and Photographs Division: pages 7, 8, 10, 12, 19, 20, 21, 25, 26, 27, 28, 29, 31, 32, 35, 42, 43; Courtesy NASA, Visible Earth Collection: pages 4, 22; Courtesy National Archives and Records Administration: pages 40, 41; Courtesy National Library of Canada: pages 12, 14, 23; Courtesy National Oceanic and Atmospheric Administration: Title Page, pages 5, 11, 24, 38, 39; Courtesy www.pdphoto.com: page 9; Courtesy Rohm Padilla: page 13; Courtesy U.S. Fish and Wildlife Service: page 15.

SPECIAL NOTE: Further information about people's names shown in the text in bold can be found on page 47. More information about glossary terms in bold can be found on pages 46 and 47.

DESIGN: ROHM PADILLA
LAYOUT/PRODUCTION: LUCY PADILLA

Library of Congress Cataloging-in-Publication Data

Thompson, Linda, 1941-
   The Great Lakes / Linda Thompson.
      p. cm. -- (Expansion of America II)
   Includes index.
   ISBN 1-59515-512-0 (hardcover)
   1. Frontier and pioneer life--Northwest, Old--Juvenile literature. 2. Great Lakes--History--Juvenile literature. 3. Great Lakes Region--History--Juvenile literature. 4. Northwest, Old--History--Juvenile literature. 5. Northwest, Old--Discovery and exploration--Juvenile literature. 6. New France--History--Juvenile literature. 7. United States--Territorial expansion--Juvenile literature. I. Title.
   F551.T48 2006
   977--dc22
                                        2005010769

TITLE PAGE IMAGE
The shores of Lake Superior

Printed in the USA

TABLE OF CONTENTS

Chapter I: A WATERWAY TO AMERICA'S HEARTLAND

Several years after **Christopher Columbus** sailed to the New World in 1492 and 1493, a few other Europeans began coming to America for "seasonal work." They were sailors from the coast of France who spent summers fishing the **shoals** of **Newfoundland**. Here, the cold ocean waters **teemed** with cod—a type of fish up to 6 feet (1.8 m) long and weighing as much as 200 pounds (91 kg). Cod could be preserved with salt after it was caught and then dried or pickled and sold when the men returned to France.

Area around Newfoundland

QUEBEC

Jacques Cartier Passage

NEWFOUNDLAND

Gulf of St. Lawrence

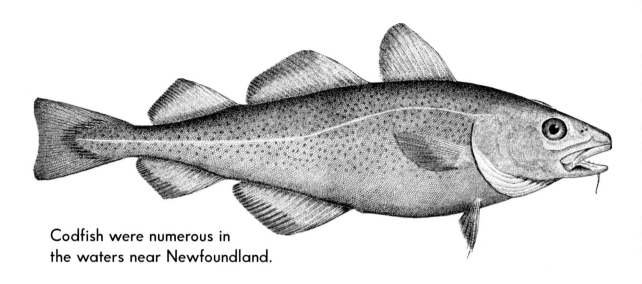

Codfish were numerous in
the waters near Newfoundland.

A good summer's catch could support a fisherman and his family for the rest of the year. Soon, **Basque**, English, and Portuguese fishing boats could also be seen on the Newfoundland coast.

Fishermen off the shores of Newfoundland

A Viking ship, from an old tapestry

From northwest France, the shores of North America are only about 2,500 miles (4,023 km) away. Columbus traveled almost twice that far—more than 4,500 miles (7,242 km)—to get from Spain to the Bahamas, where he first landed. So it is not surprising that northern Europeans such as the French found it easier to explore the shores of what is now Canada. In fact, 500 years before Columbus's voyages, Scandinavians known as **Vikings** had also visited the North American coast and even tried unsuccessfully to settle there.

French fishermen generally did not keep **ship logs**, but their reports of the new land quickly reached the ears of their king, **François I**. Increasingly worried about Spain's growing power in the Americas, he sent an Italian explorer, **Giovanni da Verrazano**, across the sea in 1523. Verrazano was supposed to establish a claim to North American lands and also look for a water route to the Far East. Europeans were always seeking more direct ways to reach China, India, and present-day Indonesia, where they could buy valuable trade goods such as silk and spices.

Verrazano's voyage launched a short but remarkable period of harmony and cooperation between Europeans and Native Americans that was very different from the conflicts **colonists** brought to other parts of the New World. The success of "**New France**" depended on water-based travel. At one time

Giovanni da Verrazano

New France included the mighty Mississippi River and five immense lakes, which hold one-fifth of all of the fresh surface water on Earth! Today these lakes—Lake Superior, Lake Michigan, Lake Huron, Lake Erie, and Lake Ontario— are known as the **Great Lakes** of the United States and Canada.

Verrazano, however, never saw the Great Lakes or the Mississippi. He reached the Atlantic coast somewhere near present-day North Carolina and sailed to Cape Breton Island, northwest of **Nova Scotia**, before turning for home. Perhaps because of the region's heavy fogs, he had missed the doorway to a part of America that would later be fiercely fought over by Britain and France. This doorway was the **Gulf of St. Lawrence**. These places are on the eastern coast of what is now Canada.

It was up to another explorer, **Jacques Cartier**, to find this opening into the North American continent and its riches of fish, fur, timber, and minerals. In 1534, Cartier left France in two small ships. He was also searching for the "waterway to the East" and must have thought he had found it when he sailed into the Gulf of St. Lawrence. He explored its shoreline, installed a large cross to claim the region for François I, and sailed home. Returning in 1535 with three ships and a hundred men, he moved up the **Fleuve St.-Laurent**, or St. Lawrence River. The river leads to a magnificent system of waterways that would prove extremely important to American trade and industry, but as Cartier probably realized, it did not lead to the Far East.

Jacques Cartier and his men erect a cross at a native village.

A typical glacier in Canada

ORIGIN OF THE GREAT LAKES

The five Great Lakes exist because of ice. More than a million years ago, enormous **glaciers** covered the land. They were as thick as 6,500 feet (2,000 m). Their weight depressed the soil where rivers had existed before the glaciers crept southward from the North Pole. About 12,000 years ago, as the earth's climate warmed, the glaciers retreated toward the north. Large amounts of melted water from the glaciers collected in the depressions, forming the lakes, and ran in different channels, forming the rivers that flow out of or into these five lakes.

Jacques Cartier with natives at Hochelaga, now Montreal

He landed at an Indian village called **Stadacona** and decided to spend the winter there. This would become the site of **Quebec**, the oldest city in Canada. Cartier also explored further upriver and exchanged gifts with natives at the site of the present-day city of Montreal. The natives somehow communicated with him, describing an immense world of water—the Great Lakes—further to the west.

A FEW GREAT LAKES FACTS

The total amount of water in the five Great Lakes is about six **quadrillion** gallons (22,710,000,000,000 kiloliters). If it were spread evenly across the lower 48 states, this water would stand about 9.5 feet (2.9 m) deep. The Great Lakes cover more than 94,000 square miles (243,460 sq km), and drain an area twice that size. Lake Superior contains 10 percent of the earth's fresh water and (by surface area) is the largest freshwater lake in the world (31,700 square miles/82,100 sq km). Including the islands they contain, the Great Lakes have more than 10,000 miles (16,090 km) of coastline. Canada and the United States share four of the lakes, with only Lake Michigan lying entirely within the United States.

The sun sets on Lake Michigan.

Samuel de Champlain (above).
Title page of Champlain's 1632 account (below)

Cartier and others made a few more voyages to North America, but it was not until 70 years later, in 1604, that **Samuel de Champlain** confirmed French claims to the region. He was a geographer sent by a religious leader, **Pierre du Guast**, **Sieur de Monts**, to found a permanent colony for the **Huguenots**. Champlain would later be called "the father of New France."

LES
VOYAGES
DE LA
NOVVELLE FRANCE
OCCIDENTALE, DICTE
CANADA.
FAITS PAR LE S DE CHAMPLAIN
Xainctongeois, Capitaine pour le Roy en la Marine du
Ponant, & toutes les Defcouuertes qu'il a faites en

The Huguenots were a **sect** of the Protestant church seeking religious freedom in the New World. Champlain chose a site for them in present-day Nova Scotia, which they called **Acadia**. Three years later he founded the settlement of Quebec next to Stadacona. From 1609 to 1615, Champlain traveled on the St. Lawrence River and connecting waterways to what is now Lake Champlain in New York. He also explored westward to Lake Ontario and Lake Huron.

Champlain's first voyage

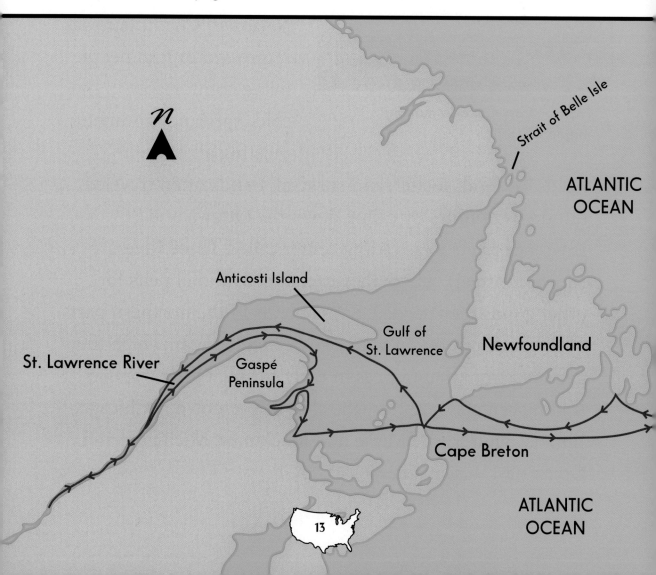

n

Strait of Belle Isle

ATLANTIC OCEAN

Anticosti Island

Gulf of St. Lawrence

Newfoundland

St. Lawrence River

Gaspé Peninsula

Cape Breton

13

ATLANTIC OCEAN

Natives from Canada making maple sugar

At that time, about 120 **bands** of **Native Americans** lived in the Great Lakes region. (A tribe is made up of several bands that are related to each other through language and culture. In Canada, Native American tribes are called **First Nations**.) Champlain was impressed to find people living comfortably in the cold, harsh environment, meeting all of their needs for food, shelter, and survival. Bands often traveled hundreds of miles by canoe down the Ottawa and St. Lawrence rivers to a trading center called Three Rivers (now Montreal), where they exchanged animal pelts for other goods they needed. Some bands in the northern parts of this region brought wild rice or maple sugar, which they gathered from maple trees in early spring. Other popular trading centers were near the sites of present-day Chicago, Illinois; Sault Sainte Marie and Mackinaw, Michigan; and Green Bay, Wisconsin.

The marshes and woodlands of Agassiz National Wildlife Refuge, Minnesota

FORESTS AND BOGS

The Great Lakes region was a paradise for animals and plants, hunters, and fishermen. The southern areas supported vast stands of oak, maple, and other hardwood trees, with prairies where grass grew as high as 10 feet (3 m). In the north, evergreen trees such as pine and fir grew in the shallow, sandy soils, with many miles of bogs and marshes near water. In the forests and grasslands lived a large variety of wildlife including moose, deer, bear, wolves, foxes, mink, and other fur-bearing species. Thousands of species of birds thrived there, and about 180 kinds of fish lived in the lakes and rivers.

The Native Americans in this area belong to a larger group that **anthropologists** have called "Northeast Woodlands people." They depended to a large degree on forest products for their survival. Great Lakes bands hunted, fished, gathered wild foods, and grew some crops such as corn and tobacco. Like other Native Americans in the sixteenth century, they were very interested in European tools and objects such as needles, fishhooks, hatchets, traps, cooking pots, fabric, beads, knives, and guns. They began trading furs and skins for these things. European traders badly wanted the pelts of animals, especially beavers, because beaver hats were popular in Europe. This made the beaver a valuable creature. In the Northeast Woodlands where fur-bearing animals were plentiful, the economy revolved around this industry. The fur trade shaped the history of the Great Lakes region, which soon involved bloody wars between France and England and their Indian **allies**.

From the start, the French had developed an **alliance** with **Algonkian**-speaking tribes and the **Iroquoian**-speaking **Huron** group. In New York, Dutch colonists formed similar alliances with the five **Iroquois** nations known as the **League of the Iroquois**. When the English conquered New Netherland in 1664 and renamed it New York, those Iroquois groups transferred their loyalties to the English.

SOME GREAT LAKES TRIBES

The Great Lakes have played a vital role in the lives of Native Americans, who have lived along their shores for centuries. Most of those groups, such as the Menominee, Ojibwe (Chippewa), Ottawa, Sauk, Fox, and Potawatomi spoke languages in the Algonkian language family. The Oneida, Erie, and Huron were Iroquoian-speaking groups. The **Winnebago** or Ho-chunk, who speak **Siouan**, still live in Wisconsin. Groups from other areas moved into the Great Lakes area under pressure from the Iroquois League to the east. These groups included the Miami, Mascouten, and Kickapoo.

A Chippewa family in a birchbark canoe

THE IROQUOIS LEAGUE

In the mid-1550s, five Iroquoian-speaking tribes formed an alliance called the Iroquois League. The five tribes were the Mohawk, Seneca, Cayuga, Onandaga, and Oneida. Much later, in 1772, the Tuscarora joined the league. This alliance was well organized and had a written constitution that may have influenced the development of the U. S. Constitution.

With Champlain and after him came many other French explorers, traders, and **missionaries**. Some of the seventeenth-century explorers were **Étienne Brulé**, **Jean Nicolet**, **Pierre Radisson**, and the **Sieur des Groseilliers**. Within a few years, these adventurers had explored, traded, and developed alliances with Indians in the woodlands throughout the Great Lakes region. Native Americans taught the French survival and boating techniques, skills they needed in this often hostile environment. By the middle of the century, France had claimed the entire network of waterways from the St. Lawrence River through the Great Lakes and down the Mississippi Valley to the Gulf of Mexico.

The eventual effect of the fur trade on Native Americans was that many bands abandoned their traditional ways of making a living and became dependent on European tools and trade. They were also drawn into the political plots of their European allies. The Iroquois had always been more warlike than the Algonkian groups, and first the Dutch, then the British, took advantage of this trait to attempt to weaken French economic and political power in the region.

A Winnebago man

Chapter III: **MISSIONS, FORTS, AND TRADING POSTS**

Statue of Jacques Marquette

Christian missionaries, especially members of the Society of Jesus, or **Jesuits**, accompanied some of the early French explorers. This **Roman Catholic** order first arrived to **convert** the Huron people in 1625. The Jesuits had strict standards for new converts so, unlike other missionaries in America, they did not persuade large numbers of natives to become Christians. Nevertheless, between 1671 and 1701 the French established a chain of small missions at strategic points around the five lakes and at the gateway to the Mississippi. One of the best known of the Jesuits was Father **Jacques Marquette**, who accompanied **Louis Joliet** down the Mississippi in 1673. They are said to have been the first Europeans on the upper Mississippi River.

Each Jesuit mission usually included a trading post where *coureurs de bois* [coo-rur duh bwa] or "runners of the woods" gathered. These bold adventurers lived in the forest, often took Native American women as wives, and trapped and traded with local tribes. Military troops sometimes used the trading posts, but they were not built primarily for defense. Each fort had a small permanent population—an administrator, a few farming families, a mission, a trading post, and often a nearby Native American village. This population expanded from time to time as traders, soldiers, and missionaries who were passing through paused to rest and restock supplies.

Traders on Lake Superior

Some of the early forts were Sault Sainte Marie between Lake Superior and Lake Huron; St. Ignace Mission on Mackinac Island between Lake Huron and Lake Michigan; Fort St. Croix near the western **portage** to Lake Superior; and La Baye at the southern tip of Green Bay on Lake Michigan. In 1701, a French nobleman, **Antoine de la Mothe Cadillac** built Fort Pontchartrain on Lake St. Clair, a small lake between Lake Huron and Lake Erie. This settlement would become the city of Detroit, Michigan.

The Great Lakes region with locations of some early forts indicated

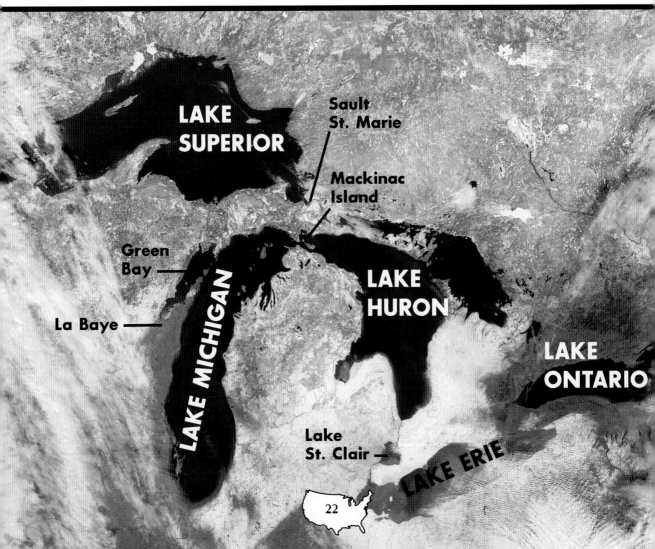

22

GREEN BAY

La Baye, which became Green Bay, Wisconsin, is the oldest settlement in Wisconsin. Champlain's lieutenant, Jean Nicolet, founded it near a Winnebago village at the mouth of the Fox River in 1634. In 1669, a Jesuit missionary, **Claude Allouez**, built a mission there. La Baye became an important rendezvous for traders, trappers, soldiers, and settlers through the eighteenth century. After the British conquered New France, they renamed the town Green Bay.

As the French extended their trading network, wars broke out between the Iroquois and the Native American groups who assisted the French. During the Iroquois

Champlain in battle during the Iroquois War

War of 1642-1653, the Iroquois managed to largely destroy the power of the Huron, Erie, Conestoga, Illinois, and a number of other French allies. They also killed hundreds of French people, including many priests. In 1666, **Jean Talon** led an army of nearly a thousand French troops to a decisive victory over the Iroquois. That defeat brought relative peace for several decades.

LA SALLE'S EXPLORATIONS

In 1668 explorer **René Robert Cavelier**, **Sieur de la Salle**, arrived in New France. He established Fort Frontenac on Lake Ontario and Fort Niagara above Niagara Falls. He is best known for traveling down the Mississippi River to its mouth in 1682 and claiming the entire region for his king, Louis XIV of France. From that voyage, the French were able to assert ownership of the huge region known as "Louisiana."

This peaceful period encouraged the French to expand into the western section of the Great Lakes region. King **Louis XIV** sent more than 950 girls to marry French soldiers and settlers. They were nicknamed "les filles du Roi" [lay feel doo rwa], or the king's girls. In 1671, a delegate of the king held a ceremony at Sault Sainte-Marie, with 14 Native American tribes attending, and claimed the entire western half of the continent for Louis XIV.

The building of La Salle's Griffon (above right)
Niagara Falls (below)

The Great Lakes and its rivers were the only practical means of moving people and freight during the colonial period. In summer, traders used 40-foot (12-m) long

birchbark canoes to bring goods such as woolen blankets, linen, copper kettles, steel knives, and beads to the trading posts. Then, using 25-foot (7.6-m) long canoes, winter traders headed up rivers and streams to buy furs from Native American villages. La Salle was the first person to experiment with boats other than canoes. He built the *Frontenac,* a small **barque** that became Lake Ontario's first sailing ship and followed it with the *Griffon,* a 40-ton (36-metric ton) **schooner** with elegant carvings. To La Salle's dismay, in 1679 the *Griffon* and its load of furs disappeared on the way to Fort Niagara. Over more than three centuries, ships and boats have played a major role in the region's history. Hundreds of them sank with their cargoes because of storms, fires, collisions, and underwater hazards.

Two forts, Pontchartrain and St. Joseph, protected the water route through Lake Ontario and Lake Erie, allowing French trading to reach southward into present-day Illinois, Indiana, and Ohio. Other forts, built from 1683 to 1703 in the river valleys to the southwest, extended French influence into Illinois country. In these fertile valleys, French settlers grew corn and other food to supply missions and trading posts to the north.

Between 1750 and 1755, New France built or rebuilt about a dozen new forts. Meanwhile, English traders and settlers were flowing into the Ohio Valley. The last two forts, Fort Le Boeuf (1753) and **Fort Duquesne** (1754, the future site of Pittsburgh, Pennsylvania), finally provoked the British. The resulting confrontation was a turning point that helped decide the fate of the Great Lakes region.

Miramichi, a French settlement on the Gulf of St. Lawrence, being attacked by British forces

Chapter IV: THE BRITISH CHALLENGE NEW FRANCE

Between 1689 and 1763, the French and British fought four wars that were at least partially about ownership of North America. After King William's War (1689-97), Queen Anne's War (1702-1713), and King George's War (1744-1748), France lost some of its power. It was also forced to give up a large amount of land in 1713, including Acadia, Newfoundland, and Hudson's Bay.

The fourth conflict, the **French and Indian War**, was the final blow for France. It lasted from 1754 until 1763 and grew into a larger conflict called the **Seven Years' War** between France, England, and other European countries. A small contingent of troops from the newly constructed Fort Le Boeuf seized an English trading post. The English governor of Virginia sent a 22-year-old lieutenant colonel named **George Washington** to western Pennsylvania to protest. But his 150 troops were defeated and he returned home.

George Washington

In March of 1754 Washington returned with 300 Virginia **militia** to build a fort at the forks of the Ohio River. In July, more than 600 French and Indian troops attacked it. Washington surrendered and was released again. The following year, the French had another victory at Fort Niagara, routing a British force attempting to take Fort Duquesne. In 1756 the war spread to Europe. In America, French troops successfully captured a number of English posts. But in 1758 the tide turned.

Fort Niagara, 1900 (above). Gun tower entrance (below)

In all of French Canada there were only about 60,000 people, compared with nearly 1 million in the English colonies. A new British prime minister, **William Pitt,** believed that unless the Canadians received heavy reinforcements from France, they could not hold out against naval attacks. The British took Quebec in 1759, and in the spring of 1760 they surrounded Montreal. In September of that year the Governor of Canada surrendered his country to England.

NAMING CANADA

In 1535 Jacques Cartier asked two Indian youths the way to Stadacona and heard the word "Kanata," which meant "village or settlement" in the Huron-Iroquois dialect. Cartier used "Canada" to refer to the entire undefined region. In 1547 everything north of the St. Lawrence River was designated on French maps as "Canada." The St. Lawrence River was called the "Riviere de Canada" until the early 1600s.

During this war the Iroquois had sided with the British, while the Menominee, Ho-chunk, Ojibwa, and Potawatomi were allied with the French. When the war ended, the British had won all of the French possessions in Canada and the Midwest. The Peace of Paris in 1763 also gave England control of the St. Lawrence, the door to the Great Lakes. In a secret treaty the year before, France had given the huge territory of Louisiana to Spain. After 1763, France was left with only a few islands off Newfoundland and in the West Indies.

When France lost its American territory, the era of friendly **coexistence** between Europeans and Native Americans came to a close. The British treated the former Indian allies of the French like conquered peoples. For example, they ended the French practice of giving supplies, ammunition, and payments to Native American leaders to ensure their cooperation. They stopped supplying rum, which many natives had become dependent upon. Instead of seeing themselves as respected partners of the Europeans, Native Americans began to feel exploited. One result was **Pontiac's Rebellion** in the Ohio Valley in 1763.

THE FRENCH INFLUENCE REMAINS

Nearly 250 years after the fall of Montreal, French is still the main language of the Canadian province of Quebec. The Acadians, banished by the British from Nova Scotia in 1755, scattered from Maine to Georgia, with most of them finally settling around New Orleans. French is still spoken there, and **"Cajun"** traditions remain strong. French place names throughout the Great Lakes region are a reminder of the colonial heyday of the French in America.

A Cajun man in Louisiana

A view of Quebec from the southeast

Chief **Pontiac** of the Ottawa people led a number of Native tribes against the British. He hoped to drive them out of the Great Lakes region and return control to the French. Pontiac's forces attacked and captured many British forts, including those at the **Straits of Mackinac**, but they failed to take Montreal or **Detroit**. But after the French and Canadians refused to join his rebellion, it lost its intensity. By 1765 the British had managed to regain control of the region.

Pontiac's warriors attacking a British fort

Old Fort Detroit

THE FOUNDING OF DETROIT

Antoine Laumet de la Mothe Cadillac, a French military leader and trader, was in charge of **Fort Michilimackinac** on the Strait of Mackinac (now in Michigan) from 1694 to 1697. In 1698, Cadillac asked King Louis XIV to let him establish a French outpost along *le detroit* ("the strait"), a waterway connecting Lakes Erie and Huron. In 1763, Fort Detroit was one of few posts that withstood a months-long siege by Chief Pontiac's forces. Detroit was a strategic British military post during the American Revolutionary War (1775-1783). But after the war ended, the British refused to give up Detroit and other western outposts. On July 11, 1796, U.S. soldiers took Detroit from the British, and the Michigan Territory became part of the United States.

Chapter V: THE NORTHWEST TERRITORY

Pontiac's Rebellion taught the British that success in the Great Lakes region depended on having good relations with Native Americans. This policy paid off when the **American Revolution** began in 1775, and almost all Great Lakes Indians sided with the British. America gained its independence when the British surrendered in 1781 (and another **Treaty of Paris** was signed on September 3, 1783). During these negotiations, the current international boundary bisecting the Great Lakes was set. However, fearing that the new United States would take away their lands, many Great Lakes Native American groups continued to support the British.

The **Northwest Ordinance** of 1787, written for the **Northwest Territory**, was later applied to other land **acquisitions**. It stated that a territory would go from a colony with an appointed governor to self-government with an elected assembly and finally to statehood. The act provided for democratic rights, public education, and freedom of religion. The act did not allow slavery in new territories. This was a progressive piece of legislation that set an orderly course for national expansion.

However, strong alliances between Britain and many Native American groups obstructed American expansion. From the beginning, Native Americans were not considered citizens of the United States because tribes had **sovereignty**. Therefore, it was difficult for the U.S. government to demand their loyalty. Britain still held Fort Niagara and other posts on the Great Lakes and continued to engage in the fur trade throughout the region.

A map of the Northwest Territory, 1787

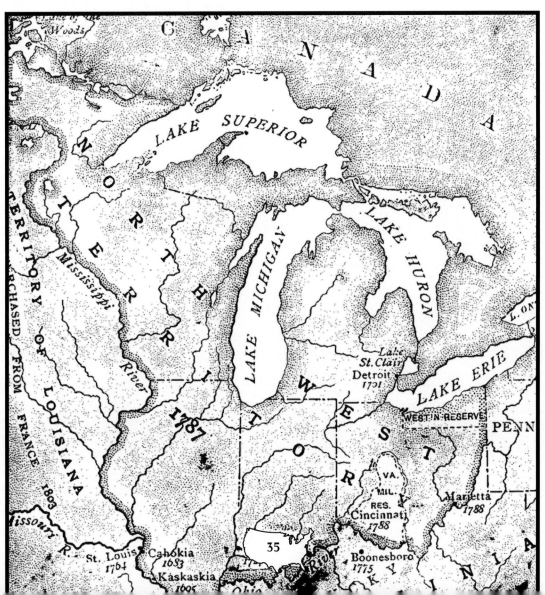

In 1791, 2,000 troops led by General **Arthur St. Clair**, governor of the Northwest Territory, tried to build a fort at the present site of Fort Wayne, Indiana. Native Americans carried out a surprise attack and killed more than 900 men. The United States tried to persuade Britain to give up trading posts in the Northwest Territory, but Britain refused. Finally, in 1794, Major General **Anthony Wayne** led several thousand troops up the Maumee River. Nearly 2,000 Miami, Shawnee, Ottawa, Chippewa, Potawotomi, Sauk, and Fox, along with 70 Canadian rangers, faced Wayne's forces at the **Battle of Fallen Timbers**. The place was named for a stockade of **felled trees** south of present-day Toledo, Ohio, behind which the Native Americans made their stand.

Wayne's forces were victorious and went on to destroy Native American villages and crops. In the **Treaty of Greenville** of 1795, Native Americans gave up huge areas of land in the southeastern Great Lakes region. This treaty opened up the Northwest Territory for U.S. settlement. Subsequent treaties with Native Americans in 1807 and 1819 saw most of the remaining tribes either confined to small reservations or pushed out of the region altogether.

General Anthony Wayne and his troops at the Battle of Fallen Timbers

MINERAL RICHES

On the shores of Lake Superior, Native Americans mined copper for centuries before French explorers arrived. Other minerals that occur in significant amounts in the region are lead and iron. However, Native American claims to minerals were lost when the Chippewa (Ojibwe) and the Sioux made peace with the United States and established a boundary line in the **Treaty of Prairie du Chien** in 1826. One clause of the treaty said, "The Chippewa tribe grants to the government of the United States the right to search for, and carry away, any metals or minerals from any part of their country."

Ore carriers (above) on the Great Lakes
Iron ore carrier (below) on Lake Superior

The United States would engage Britain once more in the War of 1812. One reason was that England had a history of **impressing** sailors from other nations on the high seas— forcing them to leave their ships and join British crews—and also sometimes taking **cargoes.** War was also seen as a way to end British support of western Native tribes, which was impeding American expansion. President Thomas Jefferson had acquired the immense Louisiana Territory from France in 1803 and wanted to make it safe for new settlers.

THE BEGINNINGS OF CHICAGO

Chicago lakefront

One area the U.S. government received in the Treaty of Greenville was a swampy piece of land on Lake Michigan near a river that Native Americans called "Checagou." In 1803, the army built Fort Dearborn on this site. About 100 people lived in the area until the War of 1812, when 400 Potawatomi warriors, agents of the British, massacred some of the inhabitants and burned the fort. Some years later, the city of Chicago arose on the site and was incorporated in 1837.

The Battle of Lake Erie

The war was fought on land, mostly around the Great Lakes region, and at sea. England was the stronger force until 1814, when the tables turned. Several decisive battles put the British on the defensive, and the **Battle of Lake Erie** was a turning point. However, several months later, British troops marched to the U.S. capital, Washington, D.C., and burned many public buildings. The war ended in favor of the United States when troops led by General **Andrew Jackson** won a number of battles in the southern states.

On January 8, 1815, he defeated the British navy, including more than 2,000 men, at the **Battle of New Orleans**. This victory gave

Signing the Treaty of Ghent

Americans much needed national pride, even though a peace treaty, the **Treaty of Ghent**, had already been signed by negotiators in Belgium on December 24, 1814.

The Battle of New Orleans

The Erie Canal at Salina St., Syracuse, around 1900

New York State's completion of the **Erie Canal** in 1825 triggered a development boom in the Great Lakes region. Shipping costs plunged, and it became much easier for settlers to travel from New York City inland to Cleveland or Detroit. When railroads were built from Chicago to the Mississippi River in the 1850s, that city surpassed Detroit as a magnet for **immigrants** and industry.

As westbound settlers filled the Great Lakes region in the second half of the nineteenth century, massive changes occurred. The new residents cut the forests, overfished the waterways, and plowed the land for farming. The wastes from timber cutting clogged streams and rivers. As the human population grew, wildlife numbers sharply declined. The development of industry caused chemical pollution of lakes and rivers. Also, excessive fishing caused a breakdown in the food chain, while uncontrolled farming exposed soil, leading to erosion and loss of fertility. During the last half of the twentieth century, laws were passed to regulate pollution. Gradually, the forests, fish habitat, and soil of the region began to make a recovery.

As for the Native Americans of the Great Lakes region, the United States pursued a policy called "Indian removal." Many tribes were sent west across the Mississippi or were driven to new lands in Kansas and Oklahoma. Some Potawatomi refused to go and instead moved to northern Wisconsin. About half of the Ho-chunk, as well as the Menominee and the Ojibwe, also refused to leave.

In spite of all of the wars and violence, the United States and Canada, which is now an independent country in Britain's **Commonwealth**, periodically celebrate the long current period of peaceful cooperation. In a few years, the Treaty of Ghent will be two centuries old. On June 26, 1959, President Dwight D. Eisenhower dedicated the U.S.-Canadian "St. Lawrence Seaway," which allowed large oceangoing vessels access to use the Great Lakes, calling it "a magnificent symbol" of the enduring friendship of two nations.

Loading a freighter on the Great Lakes with coal

A Timeline of the History of
THE *Great* LAKES

CE 1000   Leif Eriksson, a Viking, sails to the coast of what is probably Newfoundland.

1492   Christopher Columbus lands on an island in what is now the Bahamas, opening the door to European immigration to America.

1523-24   Giovanni da Verrazano explores the coastline of present-day Canada, establishing a French claim to North America.

1534-35   Jacques Cartier explores the Gulf of St. Lawrence and the St. Lawrence River.

1604-1608   Champlain arrives in the New World, founds Acadia for the Huguenots, and establishes a trading post at Quebec.

1625   Jesuit priests arrive in New France to convert the Huron people.

1634   Founding of La Baye, later Green Bay, Wisconsin.

1642-1653   Iroquois War, in which the Iroquois wipe out Native American allies of France.

1666   Jean Talon leads French troops to victory over the Iroquois.

1673   Father Jacques Marquette and Louis Joliet explore the upper Mississippi River.

1682   La Salle claims the entire Mississippi River watershed for France.

1683-1755   The French build a chain of forts reaching to the Mississippi.

1701	Cadillac builds Fort Pontchartrain, later Detroit.
1713	Queen Anne's War, after which the French lose Acadia, Newfoundland, and Hudson's Bay to Britain.
1754	The construction of Fort Duquesne (later Pittsburgh) provokes British attacks.
1754-1763	The French and Indian War, resulting in France losing all American possessions except for a few islands to Britain.
1755	The British banish the Acadians ("Cajuns") from Nova Scotia.
1763-1765	Chief Pontiac's Rebellion.
1776-1783	The American Revolution.
1787	Congress passes the Northwest Ordinance.
1791-1794	Series of skirmishes between British-allied Native American groups and U.S. settlers and troops, ending with U.S. victory in the Battle of Fallen Timbers.
1795	Treaty of Greenville opens up formerly Native American lands for American settlement.
1803	President Thomas Jefferson purchases Louisiana Territory from France. The Army builds Fort Dearborn, later Chicago.
1812-1814	The War of 1812, ending with the Treaty of Ghent on December 24, 1814.
1815	The Battle of New Orleans.
1825	The Erie Canal opens between Albany and Buffalo, New York, making the Great Lakes region more accessible.

GLOSSARY

Acadia - Early French settlement for the Huguenots in Nova Scotia, Canada.

acquisition - Something gained.

Algonkian - Language of related groups of Native American people who were widely distributed around North America.

alliance - Bond or connection; friendship.

ally - A person or group that associates with another to promote common interests.

American Revolution - (1775-1781) The war that established the independence of the 13 American colonies from Britain.

anthropologist - A person who studies human beings in relation to their environment, social relations, and culture.

band - Group of Native Americans that makes up a subdivision of a tribe.

barque - French word for a small boat propelled by sails or oars.

Basque - Describes a people who live in the Pyrenees Mountains in southern France and northern Spain.

Battle of Fallen Timbers - Two-hour engagement in 1794 in which General Anthony Wayne defeated the Ohio Native Americans.

Battle of Lake Erie - War of 1812 battle in which Commodore Oliver Perry defeated British fleet near Put-in-Bay, Ohio.

Battle of New Orleans - The last battle in the War of 1812, in which General Andrew Jackson defeated the British, with 2,500 British casualties.

Cajun - From "Acadian," a Louisiana descendent of immigrants from Acadia.

cargo - The goods carried in a ship, airplane, or vehicle.

coexistence - Living in peace with each other as a matter of policy.

colonist - A person who establishes a colony or settles a new land or region.

Commonwealth - Great Britain plus more than 45 other sovereign states, including Canada, that once were part of the British Empire.

convert - To convince a person to change beliefs; a person who has changed from one belief to another;

Detroit - City in southeast Michigan founded in 1701 as Fort Pontchartrain.

Erie Canal - Historic waterway built in New York State to connect the Hudson River with Lake Erie.

felled trees - Trees that have been cut or knocked down and are on the ground.

First Nations - Canadian term for Native American tribes.

Fleuve St.-Laurent - French for "St. Lawrence River."

Fort Duquesne - French fort built in 1754 on the site of present-day Pittsburgh.

Fort Michilimackinac - Fort built by the French in 1712-1720 to guard the Straits of Mackinac.

French and Indian War - A series of wars in North America from 1754 to 1763 between British and French colonists and their Native American allies.

glacier - A large body of ice moving down a valley or spreading out on a land surface.

Great Lakes - Five interconnected freshwater lakes between Canada and the United States; they are Lakes Superior, Michigan, Huron, Ontario, and Erie.

Gulf of St. Lawrence - Broad, deep gulf in the Atlantic Ocean between Newfoundland and the eastern coast of mainland Canada.

Huguenot - French Protestant group of the 16th-18th centuries.

Huron - Iroquoian-speaking Native American group that allied with the French and were nearly wiped out by the Iroquois League; now called the Wyandot, they live in Kansas and Oklahoma.

immigrant - A person who moves into a country from somewhere else.

impress - To force into service, especially naval service.

Iroquoian - A Native American language family of eastern North America.

Iroquois - A Native American person who speaks Iroquoian and shares the culture of this group.

Jesuit - A member of the Roman Catholic Society of Jesus founded by Ignatius Loyola in Spain in 1534.

La Baye - French for "the bay," early name of Green Bay, Wisconsin.

League of the Iroquois - An alliance of five tribes—the Mohawk, Seneca, Cayuga, Onandaga, and Oneida—formed about 1570 in the region of New York State, Ontario, and Quebec.

militia - A body of citizens organized for military service.

missionary - A person undertaking a mission, especially a religious mission.

Native American - A member of the first peoples of North America.

New France - French colony in North America that once included Quebec, Ontario, and the Newfoundland region in Canada, and reached into today's U.S. Great Lakes region.

Newfoundland - Large province of eastern Canada on the Atlantic Ocean.

Northwest Ordinance - U.S. law of 1787 that described when settled land could become a territory or a state and defined the rights of people living there.

Northwest Territory - Also known as the "Old Northwest," the region north of the Ohio River, east of the Mississippi, and including the southern and western shores of the Great Lakes.

Nova Scotia - Province in Canada on the Atlantic Ocean.

Pontiac's Rebellion - War led by Chief Pontiac of the Ottawa Natives against the British in the Great Lakes region in 1763-1766.

portage - The route followed in carrying boats or goods overland from one body of water to another or around an obstacle such as a rapids.

quadrillion - One thousand trillions; 1,000,000,000,000,000.

Quebec - Canada's oldest city and the capital of Quebec province.

Roman Catholic - A Christian church with priests and bishops under the authority of a pope.

schooner - A sailing ship with two masts.

sect - A group (usually religious) with a specific doctrine and a leader.

Seven Years' War - (1756-1763) A worldwide conflict growing out of the competition between France and England for an overseas empire, and also involving Austria, Prussia, and Russia.

ship log - The record of a ship's speed or of her daily progress.

shoals - Shallower waters, specifically six fathoms (36 ft/11 m) or less where the bottom is sandy.

Siouan - A family of Native American languages that is the main language family on the Great Plains.

sovereignty - Independent power or freedom from outside control.

Stadacona - Name of the Native American village near the site of Quebec where French explorer Jacques Cartier wintered in 1535-36.

Straits of Mackinac - Connecting waterway between Lake Michigan and Lake Huron, which was of great strategic importance to the defense of the upper Great Lakes.

teem - To be present in large quantity.

Treaty of Ghent - Treaty of 1814 signed by the United States and Great Britain in Ghent, Belgium, ending the War of 1812.

Treaty of Greenville - Agreement signed in 1795 by Native Americans of Ohio and Indiana after their defeat by U.S. General Anthony Wayne at the Battle of Fallen Timbers.

Treaty of Paris of 1783 - Agreement between the United States and Great Britain that ended the Revolutionary War and resulted in American independence.

Treaty of Prairie du Chien - Treaty made in 1826 between the United States and a number of Native American groups, including the Sioux and the Ojibwe (Chippewa).

Viking - Member of a group of Scandinavian pirates who roamed the seas in the 10th and 11th centuries.

Winnebago - Siouan-speaking Native American group that lived on the shores of Lake Michigan; small groups remain in Nebraska and Wisconsin.

Key People in the History of THE GREAT LAKES

Allouez, Claude (1622-1689) - Early French missionary in Canada.

Brulé, Étienne (1591-1633) - French explorer who came to Quebec in 1608 with Samuel de Champlain.

Cadillac, Antoine de la Mothe (1658-1730) - French colonial administrator who founded Detroit in 1701.

Cartier, Jacques (1491-1557) - French explorer sent by François I to find a northwest passage to the Far East.

Champlain, Samuel de (1567-1635) - French explorer and founder of New France.

Columbus, Christopher (1451-1506) - Italian explorer in the service of Spain who discovered America for the Europeans in 1492.

François I (1494-1547) - King of France 1515-1547.

Groseilliers, Sieur des, Médard Chouart (1618 - 1710) - A *coureur de bois*, one of the first Europeans to penetrate deep into the forests of the Great Lakes region.

Jackson, Andrew (1767-1845) - Seventh president of the United States (1829-1837).

Joliet, Louis (1646-1700) - French-Canadian explorer, one of first on the upper Mississippi River.

La Salle, René Robert Cavelier, Sieur de (1643-1687) - French explorer in North America. Explored the Mississippi to its mouth and claimed the land for Louis XIV of France (1682).

Louis XIV (1638-1715) - King of France 1643-1715, known as the "Sun King."

Marquette, Jacques (1637-1675) - French Jesuit missionary and explorer in America.

Monts, Pierre du Guast, Sieur de (1560?-1630?) - French Huguenot explorer and colonizer in North America.

Nicolet, Jean (1598-1642) - French explorer in North America; the first European to explore the western Great Lakes.

Pitt, William (1708-1778) - English statesman, secretary of state (1756-1757) and head of the government 1757-1761.

Pontiac, Chief (died 1769) - Leader of the Chippewa, Potawatomi, and Ottawa tribes.

Radisson, Pierre (1636-1710) - Brother-in-law of the Sieur des Groseilliers, helped explore the upper reaches of the Mississipi and Missouri rivers.

St. Clair, Arthur (1736-1818) - Governor of the Northwest Territory 1787-1802.

Talon, Jean (1625-1694) - French colonial leader in Canada, 1665-1668 and 1670-1672.

Verrazano, Giovanni da (1480?-1527) - Italian explorer in the service of France, who explored the Atlantic coast of North America and discovered the Hudson River, 1524.

Washington, George (1732-1799) - First president of the United States (1789-1797).

Wayne, Anthony (1745-1796) - U.S. general called "Mad Anthony" because of his daring, defeated the Ohio Indians in the Battle of Fallen Timbers (1794).

INDEX

Books of Interest

Boekhoff, P.M. and Stuart A. Kallen. *Native Americans of the Great Lakes (North American Indians)*, KidHaven Press, 2003.

Ferry, Steven. *Quebec (Exploring Canada)*, Greenhaven Press, 2002.

Marquette, Scott. *The War of 1812 (America at War)*, Rourke Publishing Group, 2002.

Maestro, Betsy. *Struggle for a Continent: The French and Indian Wars 1689-1763 (The American Story)*, HarperCollins, 2000.

Moore, Christopher. *Champlain*, Tundra Books, 2004.

Web Sites

Geology and hydrology of the Great Lakes:
http://www.epa.gov/glnpo/atlas/glat-ch2.html

All about the Great Lakes region:
http://www.canadainfolink.ca/glks.htm

Native American groups of the Great Lakes region:
http://www.great-lakes.net/teach/history/native/native_1.html

---

Linda Thompson is a Montana native and a graduate of the University of Washington. She was a teacher, writer, and editor in the San Francisco Bay Area for 30 years and now lives in Taos, New Mexico. She can be contacted through her web site,

http://www.highmesaproductions.com